EARLY THEMES

Apples, Pumpkins and Harvest

Ready-to-Go Activities, Games, Literature Selections, Poetry, and Everything You Need for a Complete Theme Unit

by Ann Flagg

SCHOLASTIC
PROFESSIONAL BOOKS

NEW YORK • TORONTO • LONDON • AUCKLAND • SYDNEY

To my mother, Dee Hempler,
who planted seeds of love and creativity
in my heart that I harvest every day.

Edited by Joan Novelli
Cover design by Vincent Ceci and Jaime Lucero
Cover art by Jo Lynne Alcorn
Interior design by Solutions by Design, Inc.
Interior illustration by Abby Carter

ISBN 0-590-03316-6

Contents

About This Book

Red sweet apples and round orange pumpkins are as inviting as autumn itself. If autumn makes you feel like celebrating, this book will provide a bushelful of ideas to help you sow meaningful learning across the curriculum. Launch your unit by growing a classroom crop that children plant on Monday and harvest on Friday. Explore fruits and vegetables as you launch your theme and munch on stems, roots, and leaves! Then take a close-up look at everyone's favorite fall fruit, apples and pumpkins. In the apple and pumpkin sections, you'll find fresh ideas for teaching about plants, life cycles, and everyday uses for apples and pumpkins.

Expand children's understanding with activities that explore harvest in our everyday lives. They'll journey across the United States to discover where important products originate, make peanut butter, and more. Close the unit with a celebration that allows children to showcase their learning in meaningful ways. Like a farmers market in fall, *Early Themes: Apples, Pumpkins and Harvest* is spilling over with ideas that will encourage children to make connections, build understanding of key concepts, and view autumn from a fresh and deeper perspective.

WHAT'S INSIDE?

Think of this book as a teacher's toolbox. The material is entirely flexible—you can use the ideas as they appear or incorporate them into the harvest unit you've enjoyed teaching for years. Among the tools you'll find inside are:

◎ suggestions for setting up and maintaining a learning center.

◎ appealing cross-curricular lessons about harvest, including activities, experiments, journal starters, and literature connections

◎ suggestions for journal entries that double as evaluation tools.

◎ a reproducible mini-book, plus a read-aloud story.

◎ science notes that give you important background information.

◎ age-appropriate reproducible activities, journal pages, and patterns.

◎ suggestions for planning a harvest festival that doubles as a way to wrap up your unit.

◎ a full-color poster that invites children to explore the life cycle of an apple tree.

WHY TEACH WITH THEMES?

Themes are naturally holistic. A good theme study pulls together a collection of activities that address all facets of child development, from language development to social skills. For example, in *Early Themes: Apples, Pumpkins, and Harvest*, children will measure the circumference of a pumpkin, share an apple story, and write journal entries from a pumpkin's point of view. They'll participate in movement and finger plays that enhance physical development and design a harvest quilt that promotes aesthetic development. While working together in small groups to make peanut butter and cooperating with one another to play a harvest game, children will develop social and emotional skills.

Themes integrate the foundational skills you're required to teach and help you to maximize use of time for student learning. As students participate in harvest activities, they'll be involved in science, math, and language arts simultaneously. For example, while children explore pumpkins, they'll measure them (math), brainstorm descriptive words (language arts), experiment with sink and float (science), and capture a pumpkin's texture by making rubbings (art). Children revisit concepts as one activity builds on another, deepening their understanding and strengthening skills. In this way, teaching with themes also increases retention of important concepts. For example, children will make connections when they discover that all fruits have seeds and then study the life cycle of apples and pumpkins. Themes allow you to explore a few topics in depth—letting children avoid information overload and enjoy and appreciate learning. The result? Learning is meaningful, applicable, and fun for your students and for you.

GETTING STARTED

Suggestions to help you plan, manage, and teach your unit follow.

Materials

Each lesson plan lists materials you'll need. Take a look around the classroom to see what you have on hand. To make gathering materials easier and less expensive, you may wish to send a note home, sharing information about the theme and opportunities for parent involvement. In the letter, request that parents contribute materials and produce—for example, apples, pumpkins, or other harvest items called for in an activity.

Assessment

The activities in this book provide many opportunities for children to participate in discussion, respond to literature, create projects, explore topics in greater depth at a learning center, and more—all wonderful opportunities to assess learning.

Before introducing the harvest theme, give each child a folder. Children can write their names on the outside and decorate their folders with harvest pictures. Invite children to visit their folders often and place examples of their best work inside. Use the folders to store journal entries, creative writing,

artwork, and reproducible activity sheets. At the end of the unit, the folders will offer a wealth of evidence of student learning. Share folders at parent-teacher conference time. Parents appreciate concrete examples of progress like those found in a unit folder.

During the unit, maintain your own folder for storing observations of children at work. A simple way to make sure you're observing everyone is to set up a page like the one shown here. Focus on one student at a time and jot notes inside each child's square. This method allows you to make sure you've observed every child at least once.

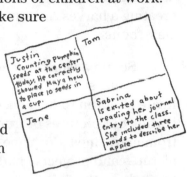

SETTING UP A LEARNING CENTER

A bale of straw and a pile of pumpkins—along with a produce basket loaded with apples, gourds, and Indian corn—can transform a corner of your classroom into an inviting harvest learning center. Learning centers act as a visual focus for the theme, providing a stimulating work environment for children who want to know more and can work independently to gather information for themselves. Centers also encourage children to assist one another in various ways, giving children opportunities to work in a cooperative atmosphere. Learning centers also help you manage theme-teaching by providing a central location for storing theme materials and projects. Here's a plan for creating a harvest learning center in your classroom:

1. Set up a work space that includes a table, several chairs, and a wall space. Invite children to help decorate the center by cutting out pictures of fruits and vegetables from magazines. Continue to decorate with pictures and projects children create throughout the unit.

2. Utilize the learning center ideas in each section to rotate center activities and keep the center fresh and inviting.

3. Organize assorted art supplies in bins or shoe boxes. Encourage the children to feel at home using the materials, but ask that they keep the center organized and ready for the next visitor.

4. Gather assorted reading materials to enhance harvest learning. Look for literature selections sprinkled throughout this book. Invite children to bring books and other reading materials from home to add to the display.

5. Post a daily or weekly rotation schedule for center use. Fill in the schedule with individual student names or group names and times for use. It may be helpful to assign each group of students a vegetable or fruit name, then code the schedule to provide a visual reminder of whose turn it is to use the center.

Professional Resources

An Apple a Day: Over 20 Apple Projects for Kids by Jennifer Storey Gillis (Garden Way Publications Company, 1993). A collection of projects that utilize apples, such as games, apple wreaths, apple-head clown dolls, and an apple puzzle.

Anna's Garden Songs by Mary Q. Steele (Greenwillow, 1989). A collection of 14 poems about vegetables grown in the garden.

Great Shapes Stationery illustrated by Rusty Fletcher (Scholastic Professional Books, 1997). This collection of 50 reproducibles includes pumpkins and apples, among other popular themes.

In a Pumpkin Shell by Jennifer Storey Gillis (Storey Communications, 1993). Pumpkin projects and activities for young children.

Instructor magazine, Primary Edition (September 1997). Features a K–3 unit on harvest that introduces a variety of harvest festivals.

Learning Centers: Getting Them Started, Keeping Them Going by Michael Opitz (Scholastic, 1994). This practical guide includes management tips, scheduling ideas, suggested topics and activities, and reproducibles.

Quick and Easy Learning Centers: Science by Lynne Kepler (Scholastic Professional Books, 1995). Includes a section on the pumpkin life cycle.

Ready, Set, Grow! by Rebecca Hershey (Good Year Books, 1995). Ideas for planting a classroom garden, including directions for a no-carve jack-o'-lantern, roasted pumpkin seeds, and mini-kabobs.

United States Apple Association. For a small fee, this association will send you teaching materials about apples. Write to the USAA at P.O. Box 1137, McLean, VA 22101.

Welcome Harvest

What's the difference between a fruit and vegetable? Children discover some surprising answers with the activities in this section. You'll find introductory activities that help children differentiate between fruits and vegetables, directions for making harvest prints, and how-tos for playing a fast-moving game that teaches about edible plant parts. Then bring the harvest theme home with a crop students can plant on Monday and harvest on Friday.

SCIENCE NOTES

A fruit is the part of a plant that contains the seeds. Examples include peaches, lemons, oranges (though navel oranges do not contain seeds), cucumbers, apples, pears, grapes, green peppers, tomatoes, and pumpkins. See a few surprises on this list? Fruit serves a seed in two ways. By protecting the seeds, fruit enables species to survive. The fruit also aids in seed dispersal. As sweet, juicy fruits are eaten by animals, the seeds are scattered far and wide.

Technically, all fruits are vegetables. A vegetable is the edible part of a plant. Examples, in addition to fruits, include beets, onions, carrots, celery, lettuce, spinach, potatoes, and turnips. The science behind the difference between fruits and vegetables can be difficult for young children to grasp. At this age, it's best to focus on one concept: Fruit contains seeds.

SCIENCE/CRITICAL THINKING

Which One Doesn't Belong?

Children discover differences between fruits and vegetables in this sorting activity and learn that only fruit contains seeds.

Materials

- apple
- lemon
- cherry
- lettuce
- pear
- bell pepper
- celery
- radish
- cucumber
- tomato
- potato

Teaching the Lesson

1 Gather children together in a circle on the floor. Initiate a conversation about fruits and vegetables by asking: "What are some fruits you know? Vegetables? What makes something a fruit? A vegetable?"

2 Place an apple, pear, peach, and carrot in front of children. Explain that one of the items does not belong. Ask: "Which one do you think doesn't belong?" (the carrot) "Why?" (It doesn't have seeds.)

3 Set up the game again with the lemon, apple, lettuce, and pear. Ask: "Which one doesn't belong?" Repeat the activity with the following groups:

- lemon, bell pepper, celery, apple
- tomato, bell pepper, potato, cherry
- tomato, radish, bell pepper, cucumber

4 Cut open each item. Ask: "What do you see?" (seeds, no seeds) Have children work together to sort the produce into two groups: produce that contains seeds and produce that doesn't.

5 Work together to write a definition of fruit. For example, "A fruit is the part of a plant that contains the seed."

6 Invite children to name other fruits and vegetables that could be added to each group.

Keep sliced produce from this activity on hand for Harvest Prints. (See page 9.)

Literature Connection To help explain the difference between fruits and vegetables, read *Vegetables, Vegetables* by Fay Robbinson (Children's Press, 1994) and *We Love Fruit* by Fay Robbinson (Children's Press, 1992).

ACTIVITY Extension Introduce children to an exotic fruit: the kiwi. Pass around a kiwi and let everyone feel its skin. Invite children to suggest words that describe the skin, such as rough, furry, and brown. Cut it open and study the many tiny seeds inside. Compare the number of seeds in the kiwi to that in other fruits. Invite children to share observations. Identify the kiwi as a fruit. Make a simple two-column graph on a sheet of chart paper. Label the columns Yes and No. Title the graph "Do You Like Kiwi?" Slice several kiwis and let students taste. Have children take turns recording their preferences on the graph. Guide children in interpreting results.

Learning Center Link

Write "I like fruits and vegetables" across a large sheet of white paper. Place this paper, along with seed catalogs, in the center. Provide crayons and colored pencils. Let children draw and label pictures of fruits and vegetables they like, using seed catalogs for inspiration. Send home a note inviting families to send in some of their favorite fruits and vegetables to share with the class. As the goodies trickle in, wash and then slice each and look for seeds. Cut into pieces for students to taste. Read about them in encyclopedias, seed catalogs, and other sources.

ART/SCIENCE

Harvest Prints

Sliced fruits and vegetables make unusual stamps. Let students use produce to make realistic prints. After the prints dry, children will revisit the concept that fruits contain seeds.

Materials

◎ fruits and vegetables
◎ tempera paint
◎ foam trays
◎ white construction paper
◎ markers

Preparation

Cut cross sections of apples, peppers, carrots, potatoes, oranges, and other fruits and vegetables that produce clear prints. Place some sections that still contain seeds on paper towels and label. Prepare other sections for printing: Remove seeds from fruit. Place these fruit and vegetable sections on trays. Pour tempera paint into separate trays, matching the natural colors of fruits and vegetables as closely as possible. Set up several stations with printmaking supplies so that children can work in small groups.

CAUTION: Remind students that the fruits and vegetables they are using to make prints are not for eating.

Teaching the Lesson

1. Demonstrate how to lightly press a fruit or vegetable section into paint and then press on paper and lift up to make a print.

2. Let children make their own prints, dipping fruits and vegetables in paint that best matches their natural colors.

3. When the prints dry, have children study the corresponding samples on the paper towels that still contain seeds and draw the seeds on their fruit prints. (The prints made with vegetables will not have seeds.) This will reinforce children's understanding that only fruits have seeds.

ACTIVITY Extension Let children make more fruit and vegetable prints, using whatever colors they like. This is a good opportunity to add patterning extensions, letting children start patterns for other children to continue. You can do the same, using fruits and vegetables to start patterns for students to continue. (You can make copies of them after the paint dries to make a class set of patterns to play with.)

Literature Connection Share *Lunch* by Denise Fleming (Henry Holt, 1992), the story of a hungry mouse who eats nine fruits and vegetables and leaves little stains that have everyone guessing. Begin by reading the story. Together, write a sequel that introduces the hungry mouse to some new fruits and vegetables. Using the stamps from Harvest Prints (see page 9), have students work in groups to illustrate and write pages for a class book. One child can draw a mouse on the page, another can use a vegetable or fruit to make a print, a third can write or dictate the text. Before putting pages together, decide on the order in which the mouse will eat the fruits and vegetables. Have children use their fingertips to smudge the colors of each previous fruit or vegetable on the mouse (like the mouse in the book). Brainstorm a title for the sequel (perhaps someone will recommend *Dinner*), and add a colorful cover.

MOVEMENT/SCIENCE/LANGUAGE

Tossed Salad

Play this fast-moving circle game to teach children about edible plant parts.

SCIENCE NOTES

Plant parts and examples of each follow. Copy the list on chart paper. Encourage students to add their own ideas.

Roots: carrots, beets, radishes

Stems: celery, onions

Leaves: lettuce, spinach, cabbage

Fruits: tomatoes, oranges, grapes, cucumbers

Flowers: broccoli, cauliflower

Seeds: corn, oats, peanuts

Materials
- Tossed Salad cards (see page 13)
- crayons, markers
- scissors
- hole punch
- yarn (cut into 18-inch pieces, one per child)

Preparation
Make enough copies of the Tossed Salad pattern page so that when cut apart, each child will have one salad ingredient. Punch two holes at the top of each picture.

Teaching the Lesson

1. Give each child a salad ingredient card and a length of yarn. Have children string their cards to make necklaces. They can color the cards first if they like.

2. Write "Tossed Salad" on the board and then brainstorm ingredients for salad. As children volunteer their favorite salad ingredients, offer comments like: "You like carrots. That means you like to eat roots!" or "Stems are delicious! I like celery too."

3. Prepare to play Tossed Salad. Review the plant part each card represents—for example, when you eat a carrot, you're eating a root. (See Science Notes, left.)

4 To play the game, arrange chairs in a large circle and have children plant themselves in seats. Call out one salad item— for example, "Carrots!" Have all children wearing carrots stand and find a new chair from among the ones vacated by the other carrots. After the children catch on, announce more than one item at once: "Carrots and Tomatoes!" Finally, call out "Tossed Salad" and have everyone get up and find a new seat.

5 For a challenge, switch from the name of the fruit or vegetable to the name of the plant part. For example, call out "Stems!" or "Leaves and Flowers!" Don't forget everyone's favorite: "Tossed Salad!"

ACTIVITY Extension Lead the class in a tasty review. Serve carrot sticks, celery sticks, broccoli flowerettes, lettuce leaves, cherry tomatoes, and other plant parts. Have children name the plant parts before they crunch and munch.

Literature Connection Does the mention of raw vegetables evoke cries of *Ew!* and *Yuck!* from picky eaters in your class? *Oliver's Vegetables* by Vivian French (Orchard Books, 1995) is the story of a little boy who developed a taste for vegetables after helping his grandfather grow a vegetable garden. Share it with students and then invite them to tell their own stories about vegetables they like or don't like. Encourage children to appreciate differences in opinions among classmates.

JOURNAL Junctures Invite students to keep a list of all the plant parts they eat in a week. Guide them in using the information to make plant-part riddles, following these steps:

◎ Draw a picture of a plant part (or cut one out of a magazine or grocery store flyer).

◎ Paste it on the bottom half of a sheet of construction paper and fold the paper in half.

◎ With the fold at the top, write clues about the identity of the fruit or vegetable on the outside. (Encourage students to use prior knowledge and information gathered about fruits, vegetables, and plant parts to write their clues.)

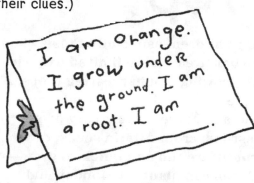

Let students share their riddles with the class—reading them aloud then adding them to an interactive bulletin board display. Children can check guesses by lifting the flaps to reveal the pictures.

Learning Center Link

Place a large plastic bowl in the harvest center and fill it with toy salad items. (Check toy and craft stores.) Provide small plastic bowls and let children pretend to make their own tossed salads.

A Classroom Crop

Many children, especially those who live in urban areas, have limited experience with growing and harvesting crops. A simple solution is to help children plant, grow, and harvest their very own classroom crop. Alfalfa seeds, or sprouts, are fun and quick to grow—children can plant on Monday and harvest on Friday!

Materials

- alfalfa seeds (check health food stores)
- 1 quart-size self-sealing vegetable bag per child (these bags have air holes)
- permanent marker
- hand lenses
- journal page (see page 14)
- brown paper lunch bags
- shallow tray or pan

Teaching the Lesson

1. Monday/Prepare the seeds: Give each child a teaspoon of alfalfa seeds inside a self-sealing vegetable bag. Write names on the outside of the bags with a permanent marker.

2. Let children use hand lenses to study the seeds. Ask them to record what they see in their Farmer's Log. (See Journal Junctures, right.)

3. Soak the bags overnight in a pan full of water.

4. Tuesday/Plant the crop: Open a bag and run fresh water over the seeds. Drain excess water by squeezing it through the holes. Dry the bag and then place it in a brown paper lunch bag. Have children do the same with their bags.

5. Wednesday and Thursday/Care for the crop: Have children care for their seeds as described above. They can also examine the seeds, look for changes with the hand lens, and record observations on their journal pages.

6. Friday/Harvest the crop: First thing in the morning, discard the brown paper bags and place the plastic bags in a sunny location such as a windowsill. Here, the sprouts will make chlorophyll and become green. Children will be able to harvest and eat their green sprouts by the afternoon.

ACTIVITY Extension Try these suggestions for serving your sprouts.

- Sprinkle fresh sprouts on peanut butter sandwiches.
- Try them on crackers with cheese.
- Bring them home to enjoy on a salad.

JOURNAL Junctures Acquaint students with the process of recording scientific observations by having them keep a farmer's log as they grow their crops. (Use the reproducible on page 14.) Beginning on Monday have students examine the alfalfa seeds, draw what they observe, and write or dictate a sentence in the boxes. At the end of the week, share the logs to review the growing process.

Literature Connection Most harvests do not come as quickly and easily as an alfalfa crop. Help children understand the work and time involved with farming. Read *Corn Belt Harvest* by Bial Raymond (Houghton Mifflin, 1996) to follow a corn crop from planting to harvest to market. Or join Mouse and Mole as they plant and tend a harvest in *Mouse & Mole and the Year-Round Garden* by Doug Cushman (Freeman, 1994).

Tossed Salad

carrot

celery

lettuce

tomato

cucumber

broccoli

JOURNAL PAGE: Farmer's Log

Farmer _____'s Log	MONDAY **Prepare the Seeds**
TUESDAY **Plant the Crop**	WEDNESDAY **Care for the Crop**
THURSDAY **Care for the Crop**	FRIDAY **Harvest the Crop!**

Apples All Around

Apples! Do you like yours red, yellow, or green? Children will discover their apple preferences and more with activities that feature everyone's favorite fall treat. They'll learn about the life cycle of an apple, make a delicious apple treat, and read a story about a little green worm that finds a special home.

SCIENCE NOTES

Crunch. If you enjoy fresh apples, you are familiar with the juicy crunch in every bite. Apples crunch because they are composed of cells that are filled with water. When you bite into an apple, the cells explode and shoot out tiny fountains of water. Why do you think oranges don't crunch? (The cell walls are soft.)

Tasting Apples

There are thousands of varieties of apples. This activity gives students a taste of three!

Materials

- ◎ crayons
- ◎ drawing paper
- ◎ Golden Delicious apples
- ◎ Red Delicious apples
- ◎ Granny Smith apples
- ◎ journal page (see page 24)
- ◎ knife and cutting board
- ◎ napkins

Teaching the Lesson

1. Provide red, green, and yellow crayons and drawing paper. Without displaying any apples, have children draw and color an apple from memory. You'll probably find that many draw red apples, a few may draw green apples, and perhaps one may draw a yellow apple. Invite children to share their drawings. Discuss the differences.

2. Display Red Delicious, Golden Delicious, and Granny Smith apples. Ask: "Which look most like the apple you've drawn?"

3. Distribute the reproducible and have children read the color words and color the apples accordingly.

4. Slice the apples and sample them with students. Guide children in finding out the class favorite, using the journal page. Call out "Golden Delicious," and ask children who prefer this apple to stand. Count together and have children color in one stick figure for

SCIENCE NOTES

In the United States more than 190 million bushels of apples are grown each year. More than half of these are eaten fresh. Fresh or in a pie, apples deliver vitamins A and C, potassium, and pectin. Characteristics and common uses of a few different varieties of apples follow.

Red and Golden Delicious: American variety; crown of five points on end opposite stem; good in pies

Granny Smith: tart and crisp; good in pies

Winesap: used for making cider

McIntosh: juicy bright red eating apple with thin skin; good for making applesauce

Cortland: named after an area in Central New York, this large red-skinned apple is great for salads (slices don't brown quickly)

each child who is standing. (If you have a large class or want to increase the difficulty of the exercise, have each stick figure represent two children. Make sure children note this in a key for the graph.) Repeat this procedure for the other two varieties. Have children write the total for each apple in the spaces to the right and then complete the sentence.

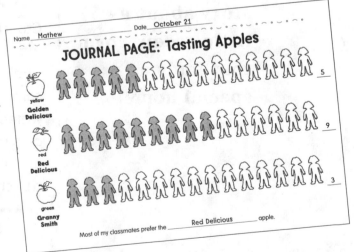

For more apple-tasting fun, set up a taste test with a selection of the shiny, attractive apples available at grocery stores as well as more unusual varieties. A good source for specialty apples is Applesource. From Arkansas Blacks to York Imperials, Applesource ships more than 100 varieties of apples. You can "pick-your-own" or choose a sampler of a dozen modern and antique varieties. For more information, call (800) 588-3854 or visit them on the Internet at www.applesource.com.

After setting up your taste-testing table, let children wear blindfolds as they taste and rate the apples. They might be surprised to find that their favorites are not quite as attractive as the apples they usually see at the store! Follow up your taste test by helping children understand the many uses for different kinds of apples. First let them suggest the things they think each variety is best-suited for. Share information from Science Notes to learn more.

Cultivate observation skills with this simple activity. Give each child an apple to examine and then draw. Have children compare these apple drawings with their earlier drawings. (See Tasting Apples, page 16.) Ask: "How are the drawings different? What details did you include in your second drawing that you did not include in the first?" Have children observe their apples once more and write words that describe them under their drawings. Invite children to share their descriptive words. Chart them according to senses: words that describe how apples smell, taste, feel, look, and so on.

Learning Center Link

Ten apples in my basket. Red and green apples! How many ways can you make ten? Provide one copy of page 25 for each child and a supply of red and green bingo daubers (stamps for marking bingo cards, available in variety stores; or cut red and green penny-size dots from construction paper). Have children stamp red and green dauber dots in and around the basket to create combinations of red and green "apples" that add up to 10. Ask children to write the resulting equation on the line below each basket. Staple students' pages together and add a child-created cover to make an apple book that shows combinations of ten.

For apple history, facts, and folklore share *The Life and Times of the Apple* by Charles Micucci (Orchard Books, 1992). The text is too advanced for young children, but they will appreciate the colorful illustrations.

Little Green Worm

Children learn more about what makes a happy home for a little green worm with this interactive story. After reading the story with children, have them retell it themselves, and then take their show on the road—sharing it at home with their families.

Materials

- *Little Green Worm Finds a Home* (see pages 26–27)
- story patterns (see page 28)
- scissors
- paper fastener
- markers
- tagboard
- sentence strips
- felt scraps
- felt board or story apron
- pear
- orange
- pomegranate
- red apple
- brown paper bag
- sharp knife and cutting board (for adult use only)
- envelopes (one per child)
- audiocassette player
- cassette tape

Preparation

Prepare for the lesson by making a copy of the patterns on page 28. Cut out and color each pattern, and mount on tagboard. Use the paper fastener to hinge the top and bottom of the apple pattern. Write the words *round, red,* *no doors, no windows,* and *star inside* on separate sentence strips. Trim each one. Attach a scrap of felt to the back of each picture and sentence strip. Prepare a flannel board (see Tip), and place the fruit in a brown paper bag.

Teaching the Lesson

1 Gather children around for an apple story. Use the felt board picture to introduce the character Little Green Worm. Read through the story, pulling each piece of fresh fruit from the brown bag as it is introduced in the story. When Little Green Worm chews through the pomegranate, slice open the pomegranate and let children observe the many seeds inside. As Little Green Worm discovers the star in the apple, cut the fresh apple as shown to reveal the star.

2 Reread the story, this time using the pictures, sentence strips, and felt board. As the worm comes to each piece of fruit, put the corresponding picture on the felt board. As you read, let children help Little Green Worm find the right home by applying Mother Worm's standard ("round, red, no doors, no windows, star inside"), placing the felt-backed sentence strips that apply to each fruit on the felt board and eliminating the pear, orange, and pomegranate when they see word cards left over (indicating that these fruits do not meet all the criteria for a good home). When Little Green Worm finds the star in the apple, open the apple and put in the worm. Children can put up all the words, indicating that this piece of fruit meets all the requirements for a "very good home."

no windows

3. Read the story a third time. Have the class participate by calling out the words on the sentence strips as you tape-record the story for the listening center.

4. During the next several days, invite children to visit the learning center to listen to the tape, using the pictures to retell the story.

5. Give each child a copy of the felt board pictures to cut out and color. When completed, store each child's pictures in a separate envelope. Let them take their pictures home and use them to retell the story with their families.

ACTIVITY Extension Most apple cores contain ten seeds. Usually, two seeds lie in each chamber of the star. Have children test the reliability of these statements. Divide the class into groups of two or three and give each an apple cut in half. Have each group draw a picture of the apple halves and do the following:

◎ Draw the seeds on the apple slices as they appear.

◎ Count the number of seeds in each chamber. Of the five chambers in each slice, how many have two seeds?

◎ Calculate the total number of seeds.

Follow up by letting children share their results. Ask: "Who counted ten seeds in their apple? More than ten? Fewer than ten?" Tally the results and then decide, based on the apples they examined, if the statement "Most apples contain ten seeds" is true or false. Try graphing the results for a visual answer

to the question. Have students tally results of the chamber seed count and then decide if the statement "Usually, two seeds lie in each chamber of the star" is true or false.

Learning Center Link

Set up a mini felt board for children to explore on their own in the learning center. Tape the sides of a file folder together, glue a piece of felt to the cover of the folder, and store the felt board pieces inside. Children can use the front of the file folder as a story mat and mini felt board. (You may wish to add a felt apple tree in one corner.)

JOURNAL Junctures Long ago people believed that the pupil of the eye was solid like an apple and the most important part of the eye. Someone who is the "apple of your eye" is an important person in your life. Let children explore other apple idioms in their journals by reflecting on what they think these expressions mean.

◎ Cheeks like apples

◎ Don't upset the apple cart!

◎ One rotten apple spoils the whole barrel.

◎ Apple pie order

Literature Connection Little Green Worm found shelter and food in an apple. Read about other animals that need the apple tree to survive in *Apple Tree* by Peter Parnall (Macmillan, 1988). Then enjoy *What's So Terrible About Swallowing an Apple Seed?*, a silly autumn story by Lerner and Goldhar (HarperCollins, 1996).

19

Learning Center Link

Cut out Little Green Worm and apple shapes for an activity that can be adapted to reinforce a variety of math or phonics skills. The object of the activity is to help each worm find its home. Use the examples here or create your own. Children will have fun making matching games to share too.

◎ *Write capital letters on the worms and corresponding lowercase letters on the apples. Have children match each worm (capital letter) with the corresponding lowercase letter form.*

◎ *Write color words on the worms. Color each apple accordingly. Have children match worms with apples—color words to actual colors.*

◎ *Write math equations on the apples and answers on the worms. Have children solve the equations, indicating their answers by placing the appropriate worm on each apple.*

◎ *Write numerals on the worms and draw the corresponding number of dots on the apples. Let children practice counting as they wiggle their worms onto corresponding apples.*

TIP: *For self-checking, write (or color) matches on the backs of the worms in each set.*

A Look at Life Cycles

Children collaborate to create a four-season display that illustrates the life cycle of an apple tree.

Materials

◎ poster (bound in back)
◎ apples
◎ chart paper and pencil
◎ apple seeds
◎ craft paper
◎ markers, crayons
◎ water
◎ glue
◎ salt
◎ tempera paint (green and yellow)
◎ tissue paper (pink)
◎ green and red construction paper
◎ scissors

Teaching the Lesson

1. Invite children to share what they know about the human life cycle. Record their comments and draw simple pictures (or cut from a magazine) to represent each stage, from infancy to old age.

2. Explain that trees have life cycles too. Ask: "What do you think the first stage of an apple tree's life cycle is?" Show children an apple seed. Explain that apple trees grow from apple seeds. Invite children to squat and pretend to grow tall like a tree, reaching their hands like branches up to the sky. Explain that once a tree is mature, it begins to grow fruit.

3. Use a black marker to draw four identical tree trunks on four pieces of

SCIENCE NOTES

An apple tree may live for more than one hundred years, but a mature tree revisits the same seasonal cycle year after year. In summer tiny buds appear on the branches. The buds develop and grow a protective covering in the fall. During the winter the buds are dormant, protected from the cold by a fuzzy coat. In the spring buds explode into green leaves and little flower buds appear. Insects pollinate the apple flowers, which give way to developing apples. Every apple contains seeds that can begin the process again. Use the poster to reinforce these concepts.

craft paper. Label them Winter, Spring, Summer, Fall. Divide children into four life-cycle groups and give each group a tree trunk. Ask: "What changes do you think happen to an apple tree in each season?" Display the poster to learn more. Review changes to an apple tree in each season. Have children in each group color in the trunks and then decorate the trees to represent each part of the life cycle. Suggestions follow.

◎ **Winter:** Use black marker and brown crayons to extend the trunk into bare branches. Paint branches with watered-down mixture of water and white glue and sprinkle with salt to create a frosty, wintry look.

◎ **Spring:** Dip an index finger in green tempera paint and make tiny leaf buds on the branches. When the paint dries, pinch pink tissue paper to make blossoms. Glue blossoms to the tree.

◎ **Summer:** Dip hands in green tempera

paint and make handprints on the branches to represent broad summer leaves. Cut out small green apples and glue them to the tree.

◎ **Fall:** Dip hands in yellow tempera paint and create handprints to represent changing autumn leaves. When the paint dries, cut out and glue on apples from red construction paper.

4 Have students in each group work together to write informative captions to go with the tree. Display trees and captions in the hall outside your classroom.

Literature Connection Learn more about the life cycle of an apple tree with *The Seasons of Arnold's Apple Tree* by Gail Gibbons (Harcourt Brace & Co., 1984). As you share the book, invite children to notice similarities between their tree murals and Arnold's apple tree.

ACTIVITY Extension Give children a close-up look at the first stages of an apple tree's life cycle by sprouting apple seeds in the classroom. Ask students to save seeds from apples they eat. Give each child a few apple seeds, a resealable plastic bag (use a permanent marker to write each child's name on the bag), and a paper towel. Demonstrate the following steps as children follow along with their materials.

◎ Moisten the paper towel with water.

◎ Fold the paper towel in half and place it inside the plastic bag.

◎ Place the apple seeds inside the bag on top of the paper towel. Close the bag partway—leaving an opening so that air can circulate inside. Lay the bag on a tray. (Bags may be stacked if necessary.)

Place the tray in a refrigerator for six weeks. (The refrigerator time simulates the long, cold winter all apples need to grow.) Bring out the trays at regular intervals and let children use hand lenses to examine the seeds through the plastic bags. (Do not remove the seeds from the bag.) Spritz the paper towels with water to keep the paper towels moist but not soggy. As the seeds begin to germinate, tiny roots and little shoots will appear. Plant the sprouts one-inch deep in paper cups filled with potting soil. Write children's names on their cups and place in a sunny spot. Have children keep the soil in their cups moist. Cover the cups loosely with plastic wrap to retain moisture and help seedlings survive over weekends.

Cooking With Apples

Turn your students into pastry chefs with this recipe for easy apple turnovers.

Preparation

Have children wash their hands. Preheat oven to 350°F.

Materials

◎ 3 cans refrigerator biscuit dough

◎ 1 can apple pie filling

◎ cinnamon and sugar mixture

◎ wax paper

◎ cookie sheets

◎ oven

◎ pencil

◎ chart paper

TIP: This recipe will make apple turnovers for a class of 25 students. Adjust for the size of your class.

Teaching the Lesson

1. To make mini apple turnovers, give each child a square of wax paper (to use as a clean work area) and a biscuit. Demonstrate the following steps as children follow along:

◎ Pat and flatten the biscuit into a 3 1/2-inch circle.

◎ Drop a slice of apple from the pie filling into the center of the biscuit circle.

◎ Sprinkle cinnamon and sugar mixture over the filling.

◎ Fold the biscuit over and pinch the edges.

◎ Place the turnovers on cookie sheets and

bake at 350°F for 10 minutes.

2 While turnovers are baking, draw a picture of an apple in the center of chart paper. Ask children to brainstorm products that are made from apples. Record their suggestions around the outside of the apple. If the list is sparse, suggest a few additional apple items, such as applesauce, apple butter, apple juice, cider, apple muffins, apple pancakes, apple pie. Discuss the versatility of the apple. Take a vote to discover students' favorite apple food.

3 Allow turnovers to cool and then let students enjoy the "fruits" of their labor!

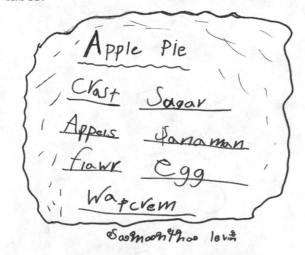

together to make a cute classroom cookbook. You can also use a copy machine to reduce recipes to fit several on a page. Collate and send this fanciful collection of recipes home for families to enjoy.

ACTIVITY Extension Invite family participation by planning an after-school apple scavenger hunt. Send a copy of page 29 home with each child. If parents donate apple items from the hunt, display them in the harvest center and allow children to taste. Can they guess the ingredients in any of the prepared items? Are there some items that also appear in the class recipe book?

Literature Connection Read *Apple Pie Tree* by Zoe Hall (Scholastic, 1996) to revisit the concept that the apples in apple turnovers were once growing on a tree. This book has simple text and collage illustrations that follow apples as they grow. If your class loved the apple turnovers, try the recipe for apple pie included in the book!

JOURNAL Junctures Ask children to review the steps for making apple turnovers. As they list the ingredients and the steps, write the information on the board so that it resembles a simple recipe. Next, have each child write a recipe to show how to make another favorite apple food. Bind recipes

Name _____

Date _____

JOURNAL PAGE: Tasting Apples

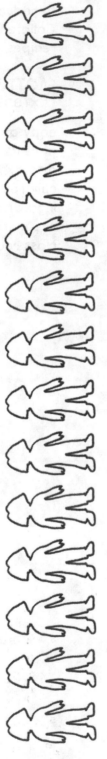

Golden Delicious — yellow

Total _____

Red Delicious — red

Total _____

Granny Smith — green

Total _____

Most of my classmates prefer the _____ apple.

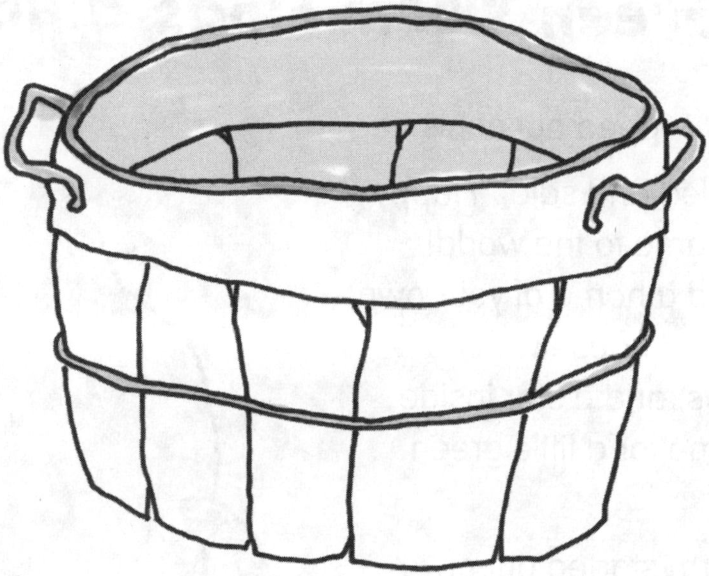

_____

_____

_____

_____

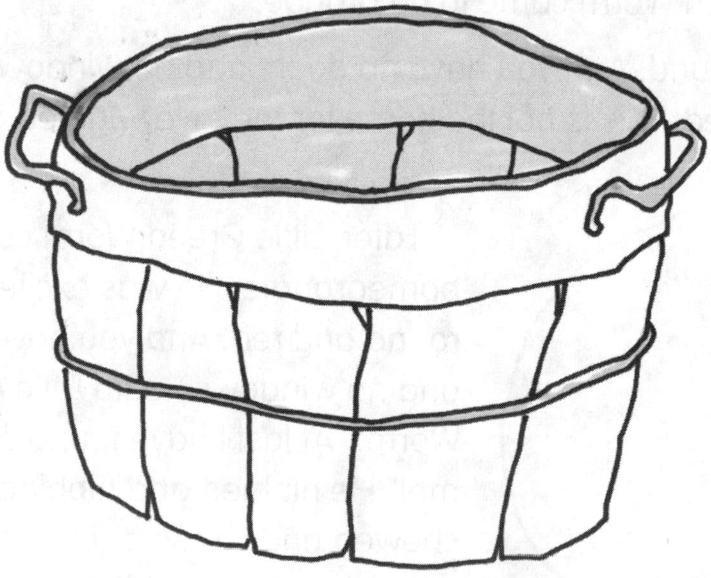

Little Green Worm Finds a Home

Little Green Worm popped out of his egg.

His mother smiled and said, "Happy birthday and welcome to the world! Now, you must find a home of your own. Look for a round, red house with no doors, no windows, and a star inside. This is a good home for a little green worm."

Little Green Worm started out on his own.

Soon he came to a pear.

"You have no doors and no windows," Little Green worm said. "But you are tall and green, not round and red. This is not the home for me." He wiggled on down the road.

Next, Little Green Worm came to an orange.

"Oh! You are round. And you have no doors and no windows. But you are orange, not red. This is not the home for me." He wiggled on down the road.

Later, Little Green Worm came to a pomegranate. He was excited! "You are round and red. And you have no doors and no windows," said Little Green Worm. "At last I have found a home for me!" He nibbled and nibbled and chewed and chewed. The skin of the pomegranate was bitter and tough but finally he found his way inside.

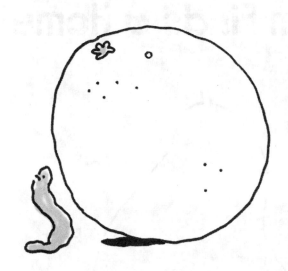

It was crowded inside! Seeds were everywhere. But no matter where he looked, Little Green Worm could not find a star. "This is not a home for me after all," he said sadly. Little Green Worm crawled out, feeling discouraged and tired. "I need a rest," he said. So Little Green Worm lay down on a golden autumn leaf under an apple tree.

Just then the wind began to blow. The branches of the tree began to sway. An apple dropped to the ground right in front of Little Green Worm. He looked at it closely. It had no windows and no doors. It was round and red. "But," wondered Little Green Worm, "is there a star inside?"

Little Green Worm began to nibble at the skin of the apple. He chewed easily through the skin. He nibbled and nibbled until he came to the core of the apple. And there, as beautiful as any star in the sky, was a star.

He cuddled close to the star and sighed, "I have found the perfect home for a Little Green Worm." And he drifted off to sleep.

Little Green Worm Finds a Home

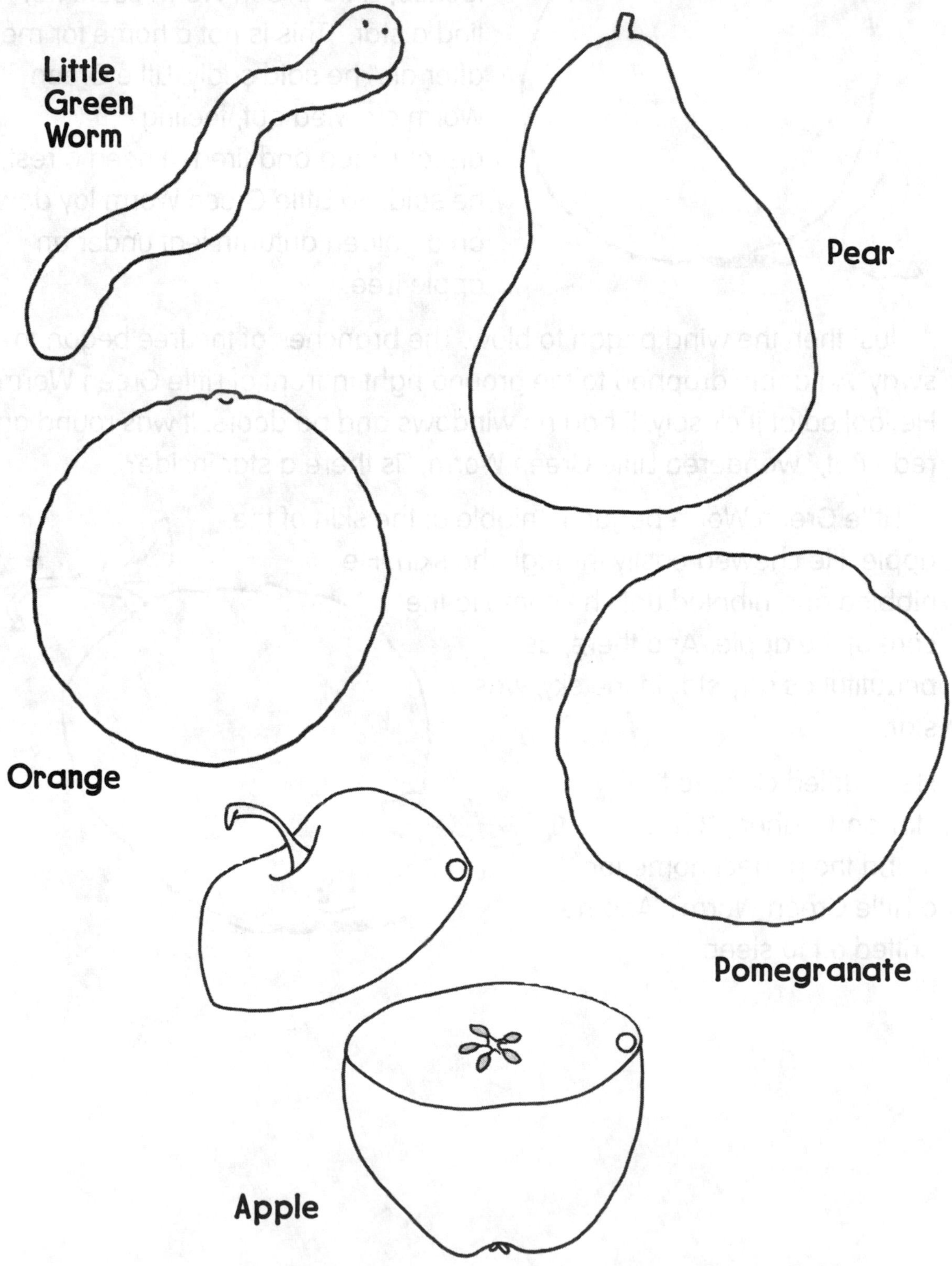

Little
Green
Worm

Pear

Orange

Pomegranate

Apple

Apple Scavenger Hunt

Dear Families,

We are learning about apples in school this week—exploring an apple tree's life cycle, cooking with apples, graphing favorite apples, sharing stories about apples, and more. To support your child's learning, try this activity together the next time you go grocery shopping. Look for the items listed. Ask your child to put a check next to as many items as you can find. Add others that aren't on the list. Feel free to send in a favorite apple food to share at our harvest center. Please return this completed assignment by _____.
Thank you.

fresh apples _____

apple butter _____

apple pie _____

applesauce _____

dried apple rings _____

apple turnovers _____

apple cake _____

apple cider vinegar _____

apple juice _____

apple jelly _____

_____ _____

_____ _____

_____ _____

_____ _____

The Pumpkin Patch

Pumpkins are a symbol of autumn plenty, and children are naturally drawn to this round orange fruit. Capitalize on their interest with the activities in this section. To start, you'll find directions for creating pumpkin stations that will have everyone exploring pumpkins inside and out. Revisit life cycles by making pumpkin vines that wind through time. Then watch together as a jack-o'-lantern decomposes and "returns to the soil." Top it off with an unusual pumpkin treat.

SCIENCE NOTES

The word *pumpkin* comes from the Greek word *pepon*, which means "large melon." The Greeks were correct in describing a pumpkin this way because pumpkins belong to the same family as melons, squash, cucumbers, and gourds!

Pumpkin Stations

Guide children in getting to know pumpkins by setting up the five stations described here. You can plan an afternoon of pumpkin fun with these stations or spread them out over a week. Either way, invite parents to staff each station and guide children in completing the activities.

Preparation
Reproduce mini-book pages for each child. (See pages 39–40.) Do not cut apart pages. (Station Five gives directions for assembling the mini-books.)

Materials
- ◎ **Station One:** one apple, one medium pumpkin, scissors, string, balance scale, pencils, chart paper, tape
- ◎ **Station Two:** medium pumpkin, colored pencils, newsprint, fat crayons
- ◎ **Station Three:** small pumpkin, large pumpkin, knife (for adult use only), glue, plastic knives, orange yarn (cut into 1/2-inch pieces), orange construction paper, roasted pumpkin seeds (optional)
- ◎ **Station Four:** plastic dishpan, water, medium pumpkin, large pumpkin (optional)
- ◎ **Station Five:** orange construction paper, crayons, scissors, stapler

----

TIP: Post "To Do" activities at each station for easy reference. Ask volunteers to use the Think About It questions to guide a discussion with each group. Children will use their mini-book pages to record information along the way.

Teaching the Lesson
STATION ONE:
Apples and Pumpkins
This station helps children make connections between apples and pumpkins, both fruits harvested in fall.

To Do
- ◎ Describe the size, shape, color, smell, and texture of the pumpkin and the apple.
- ◎ Compare the mass of the apple and the pumpkin using the balance scale.
- ◎ Measure the circumference of the pumpkin and apple by wrapping string around the widest part of each fruit.

Think About It
How is a pumpkin like an apple? How is a pumpkin different from an apple? Do you think the pumpkin is a fruit or a vegetable? (fruit) How do you know? (contains seeds)

Using the Pumpkin Book (page 1)
Record observations in the appropriate columns on page 1. Tape the apple circumference string on the apple and the pumpkin string on the pumpkin. Let the strings dangle down.

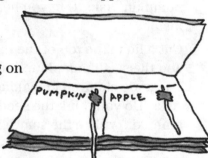

STATION TWO:
Portrait of a Pumpkin
This station invites students to slow down and observe one pumpkin to make accurate drawings.

To Do
- ◎ Observe the pumpkin. Describe the size, shape, color, scars, and markings of the pumpkin, and then draw what you see.
- ◎ Tap on the pumpkin. What do you hear?
- ◎ Place a large piece of newsprint over the pumpkin. Use a peeled crayon to make a

rubbing. Can you capture the creases in your rubbing?

Think About It

Can you tell which side of the pumpkin was on the ground when it was growing? (This side will not be as round and orange as the other.) Which side faced up? Where was the pumpkin attached to the vine? How do the creases change at the top and the bottom of the pumpkin? Where are the creases deep? Shallow?

Using the Pumpkin Book (page 2)

Use colored pencils to capture details and colors of the pumpkin. Write a few describing words about the pumpkin around the drawing.

STATION THREE:
Seeds Inside

Explore the inside of a pumpkin to learn more about seeds, fibers, and pumpkin meat.

To Do

- Invite one child to shake the small pumpkin. Ask: "Can you hear the seeds inside?"

- Cut a lid in the top of the big pumpkin and the small pumpkin. Before lifting the lid, guide children in making predictions. Ask: "Do you think the seeds in each pumpkin will be the same size, or do you think one will have bigger seeds than the other? Do you think one will have more seeds?" Lift the lids and confirm predictions.

- After everyone has had an opportunity to examine the inside of the pumpkin, let children shave off small slivers of pumpkin (not the rind) with a plastic knife and taste the raw pumpkin meat. Explain that this part of the pumpkin is what we use to make pumpkin pie.

- Collect and clean the seeds from the big pumpkin to count later. Give each child a store-bought pumpkin seed to taste.

Think About It

How are the inside and outside of a pumpkin different? How many seeds would you estimate are in each pumpkin? What keeps the seeds inside a pumpkin from rattling? (stringy fibers)

Using the Pumpkin Book (page 3)

Have each child remove several seeds from the small pumpkin, dry off the seeds, and glue them on the pumpkin picture. Glue bits of yarn to represent the pumpkin fibers. After the glue dries, children can staple a construction paper pumpkin over the pumpkin in their mini-book page to make a flap they can lift to peek inside. Estimate the number of seeds inside the large pumpkin and record it on the line below the pumpkin.

STATION FOUR:
Pumpkin Sink or Float

Predict whether a pumpkin will sink or float, and discover something surprising about such a large fruit.

To Do

Have children guess whether a pumpkin will sink or float. Ask them to complete the left side of page 4 of the mini-book to show their predictions, drawing a pumpkin below the waterline if they believe the pumpkin will sink and above the waterline if they believe the pumpkin will float. Drop the pumpkin in the water to discover that it floats. Cut a lid in the pumpkin and show children that a pumpkin is hollow inside. Explain that air trapped inside allows the pumpkin to float.

Think About It

How is a pumpkin like a boat? (For example, both are hollow inside.)

Using the Pumpkin Book (page 4)

After testing the pumpkin, have children redraw the pumpkin on the right side of the page to reflect the results of the test.

ACTIVITY Extension Repeat the activity with a larger pumpkin. Do students' predictions reflect what they learned in the first pumpkin sink-float test, or does the size of the pumpkin lead children to believe it will sink?

STATION FIVE:
Make a Pumpkin Cover

Children make covers for their pumpkin books to pull their pages together.

To Do

- ◉ Cut apart the mini-book pages.

- ◉ Use one page to trace a front and back cover on orange construction paper (6 by 9 inches). Cut them out.

- ◉ Put the pages in order. Place one orange page on the top and one on the bottom to make front and back covers. Staple the pages together. Write a title on the cover. Add the name of the pumpkin expert—you!

JOURNAL Junctures Celebrate students' discoveries. Have children gather in small groups to share books with one another.

Literature Connection Take time out for a story as children visit the pumpkin stations. *Apples and Pumpkins* by Anne Rockwell (Simon & Schuster, 1989) is the story of a trip to a farm where there is an apple orchard and a pumpkin patch. Use the book to make connections between the apple activities (see pages 15–29) and the pumpkin station activities.

Learning Center Link

Remove the pumpkin seeds from the large pumpkin at Station Three. Wash them and spread them out to dry on paper towels. As they dry, have children review the estimates they made in their pumpkin books. Provide a stack of small paper cups. Invite children to stop by the center and count out 10 seeds per cup. After all the seeds have been placed in cups, count by tens to discover how many seeds were in the large pumpkin. Compare with students' estimates.

SOCIAL STUDIES/COOKING

Pumpkin Ice Cream

Children may be familiar with pumpkins that sit lit up on porches, steps, and stoops on late October nights. But how many think of pumpkins as a food to eat? This activity invites children to stir up and sample a pumpkin treat and learn how this fruit can contribute to their health.

Materials

- ◎ 1 can pureed pumpkin
- ◎ 1 gallon vanilla ice cream
- ◎ clear plastic tumblers (one per child)
- ◎ plastic spoons
- ◎ half gallon milk
- ◎ orange food coloring

Preparation

Before class, place a scoop of vanilla ice cream in each plastic cup and freeze until you're ready to teach the lesson.

Teaching the Lesson

1. Take a quick survey. Ask: "Who likes pie? What is your favorite kind?" How many children name pumpkin? Discuss other foods made with pumpkin, such as pumpkin bread, pumpkin soup, and pumpkin butter. Then invite children to join you in making pumpkin ice cream.

2. Give each child a cup of vanilla ice cream. Add two tablespoons of milk to each cup and have children stir until the mixture is soft and resembles a thick milkshake.

3. Place a spoonful of canned pumpkin in each child's cup. Have children stir to blend the pumpkin with the ice cream. (Children who are hesitant may agree to try just a little bit. Those who absolutely refuse can add a drop of orange food coloring for color.) Then let children enjoy their frosty pumpkin treat!

 ACTIVITY Extension Help children to make a connection between canned pumpkin and the orange pumpkins they see at farm stands and in the grocery store. Purchase a cooking pumpkin. Cut it in half and have children clean out the seeds. Turn the pumpkin upside down on a cookie sheet and bake until soft. When tender, scoop out the pumpkin and blend it with as little water as necessary to make a smooth mixture. Explain that this is the pumpkin that pumpkin pies are made from. You can substitute this fresh pumpkin for canned in the recipe above.

 Literature Connection We all hold hands and sing a song
Of pumpkins round and pumpkins long,
Of pumpkins fat and pumpkins lean
And pumpkins somewhere in between.

from *The Pumpkin Fair* by Eve Bunting

Join in the rhyme and visit a pumpkin festival with *The Pumpkin Fair* by Eve Bunting (Clarion Books, 1997). There's pumpkin bowling, pumpkin tug-of-war, and a pumpkin parade! After making their own pumpkin ice cream (see Pumpkin Ice Cream, page 34), the class will be delighted to read that pumpkin ice cream was served at the fair along with some other unusual pumpkin treats! For fun, form a circle and join hands while you share the rhyme from the book. Invite children to make up movements to go with the words—for example, making the circle big and round, then long and thin.

Finally, join together for a pumpkin parade. Give each child a 12- by 12-inch piece of tagboard, and then guide them in the following steps to make pumpkin masks.

- ◉ Cut and color a pumpkin shape. Tape a craft stick to the bottom.
- ◉ Cut eye holes. (Assist children with this step.)
- ◉ Add a brown construction paper stem at the top.

With masks made, lead your patch of little pumpkins in a parade!

SCIENCE/LANGUAGE ARTS

A Vine Through Time

Capture the life cycle of a pumpkin in a foldout book children make themselves.

Materials

- ◉ white construction paper
- ◉ orange construction paper
- ◉ glue
- ◉ scissors

SCIENCE NOTES

Pumpkin vines produce male and female flowers, but the majority of flowers on a vine are male. The male blossoms have pollen that insects transfer to the female flowers. Pollinated female pumpkin flowers develop into pumpkins. Each female flower opens for pollination for only one day. As a result, very few pumpkin flowers produce pumpkins.

- ◉ brown crayons
- ◉ dry pumpkin seeds
- ◉ green markers
- ◉ yellow tissue paper (cut into 2- by 2-inch squares)
- ◉ pencil with eraser
- ◉ sponges cut into 2- and 4-inch rounds
- ◉ green and orange tempera paint
- ◉ foam trays
- ◉ black construction paper

Preparation

For each book, precut one 18- by 6-inch strip of white construction paper, two 4 3/4- by 6-inch pieces of orange construction paper, one 2- by 2-inch square of brown construction paper.

Teaching the Lesson

1. Display the poster of the life cycle of the apples and have children review the sequence. Encourage children to share what they know about the life cycle of the pumpkin. Share a book about the pumpkin life cycle (see Literature Connection, page 37) to reinforce their knowledge. Use a Venn diagram to further compare apples and pumpkins.

2 Give each child a strip of precut white construction paper. Help children follow these directions to make their books.

◎ Fold the white paper in half.

◎ Bring one half in to meet the fold.

◎ Turn the paper over. Fold the other half the same way.

◎ Attach the front and back covers by centering and gluing the orange construction paper to the exterior faces of the book.

◎ Trim the edges and add a stem to transform the rectangular book into a pumpkin-shaped book.

3 Guide children in decorating each page to represent the pumpkin life cycle.

Page 1: Color the bottom of page 1 with brown crayon to make dirt. Glue one pumpkin seed in the dirt. Use a green marker to draw a vine coming out of the seed and up through the dirt. Extend the vine along the bottom of pages 1–4. Add leaves to the vine.

Page 2: Gather a small piece (about 2 by 2 inches) of yellow tissue paper around the eraser end of a pencil. Place a dot of glue on the vine on page 2. Press the tissue-covered eraser on the dot of glue and remove the pencil to reveal a gathered, yellow pumpkin blossom.

Page 3: Dip the small round sponge in green tempera paint. Press to make a green pumpkin shape on the vine.

Page 4: Dip the large round sponge in orange tempera paint. Press to make an orange pumpkin shape on the vine.

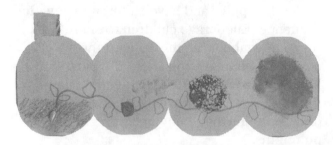

Back Cover: Have children cut shapes from black construction paper to make a jack-o'-lantern face for the pumpkin on the back cover.

Front Cover: Encourage children to write titles for their pumpkin books and add their names as authors and illustrators.

4 Guide children to recognize that each page of the pumpkin book represents a stage in the life of a pumpkin. As you review each stage, ask children to follow along in their books: The seed is planted (page 1); a pumpkin vine grows from the seed (page 1); yellow blossoms appear on the vine (page 2); the blossoms give way to tiny green pumpkins (page 3); the green pumpkins grow and turn orange in the sun (page 4); someone picks the pumpkin and carves it into a jack-o'-lantern (back cover).

ACTIVITY Extension Plant pumpkin seeds in plastic bags and start the pumpkin life cycle in your classroom! Give each child a resealable plastic bag, a paper towel, and a handful of pumpkin seeds. Then guide them in following these steps:

1. Dip the paper towel in water and wring out the excess.

2. Fold the damp paper towel to fit inside the resealable bag.

3. Place pumpkin seeds on top of the towel and seal the bag.

Use a permanent marker to write each child's name on the outside of his or her bag. Have students use thumbtacks to attach their pumpkin seed bags to a bulletin board to make a growing science display. Check the seeds daily and discuss changes.

TIP: To keep the paper towels moist, add 1/2 inch water to the bottom of each bag. The paper towel will wick the water up to the seeds.

JOURNAL Junctures Listen as children use their pumpkin books to tell the story of a pumpkin's life cycle. Children can use the space above the vine to record what they've learned about the pumpkin life cycle. Or, since writing space is limited, take dictation as children explain each page.

Literature Connection Picture books to help you teach the pumpkin life cycle follow.

It's *Pumpkin Time!* by Zoe Hall (Blue Sky Press, 1994). Beautiful illustrations and simple text show the life cycle of the pumpkin.

I'm a Seed (Hello Science Reader, Level 1) by Jean Marzollo (Cartwheel Books, 1996). Two newly planted seeds, one a marigold and one a mystery seed, discuss their changes as they grow, until the mystery seed discovers that he is a pumpkin plant!

Too Many Pumpkins by Linda White (Holiday House, 1996). This is the story of Rebecca, who grew up during the Great Depression. Pumpkins were an abundant food so Rebecca was forced to eat pumpkins daily. Years later, when a huge pumpkin falls off the back of a truck in front of her home, she quickly buries it to get the dread pumpkin out of sight. To Rebecca's surprise the seeds produce a pumpkin patch that turns dread into joy.

Learning Center Link

How does a stem do its job? Place a pumpkin and a stalk of celery in the learning center, and encourage children to analyze the stem of the pumpkin and the stalk of celery with a hand lens. Remind children that celery is a stem that we eat. Review that pumpkins grow on vines. Explain that the pumpkin was once attached to a vine at the stem. To illustrate the function of a stem, set up this simple science experiment: Pour 1/2 cup water in a jar. Add 20 drops of red food coloring. Mix. Trim the end of a stalk of celery but leave the leaves intact. Put the celery in the water. Check the celery later in the day. Ask: "What do you think happened?" (When celery grows, tubes in the stem transport nutrients from the soil to other parts of the plant. Students will observe this process as the red water moves up the celery.) "How do you think a pumpkin stem keeps a pumpkin alive?" (Like the celery stem, nutrients travel from the plant through the stem to the pumpkin, giving the pumpkin the nutrients it needs to grow. If children look at the stem, they will see the tubes that carry the nutrients.)

Return to the Soil

What to do with all the pumpkins you've collected in your investigations? Be sure to save at least one and let the life cycle wind down to its natural conclusion.

Materials

- 1 pumpkin
- knife
- shallow pan
- plastic bag to contain the seeds

Teaching the Lesson

1. Remove the seeds from a pumpkin and carve a friendly face.

2. Place the pumpkin in the pan. (Save the seeds for step 5.)

3. Observe the pumpkin for two weeks. Discuss the part of the life cycle students will observe—decomposition.

4. At the end of two weeks, find a flower bed on the school ground and deposit the pumpkin seeds and shell. Perhaps you'll find a surprise in the spring!

Literature Connection *Mousekin's Golden House* (Prentice Hall, 1964) is the story of a little mouse that takes refuge in a discarded jack-o'-lantern that he finds in the shade of a forest. As you read the story, watch the changes that occur in Mousekin's jack-o'-lantern. Compare the time it took Mousekin's pumpkin to decay to the time it took for the classroom jack-o'-lantern to decay. (Mousekin's pumpkin decays more slowly because it is in a cool environment.)

SCIENCE NOTES

Your jack-o'-lantern will last for approximately four days before rot and decay set in. Bacteria and mold are responsible for the changes in the jack-o'-lantern. Because the classroom is warm and the pumpkin is moist, these living organisms are able to digest the pumpkin over a short period of time. When it is left in the flower beds, it will blend with the garden dirt and return to soil.

JOURNAL Junctures During the two-week jack-o'-lantern watch, encourage children to use their observation skills and a little imagination to write journal entries from the pumpkin's perspective. If adapting a new point of view is too difficult, take dictation and work together to write a comment from the pumpkin's point of view each day, or simply record observations.

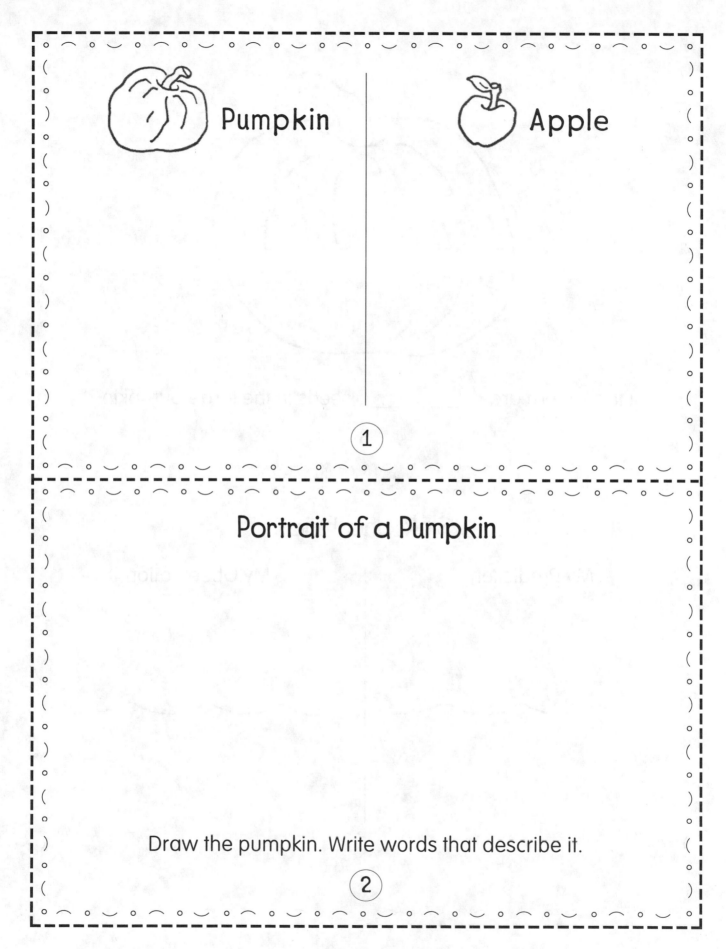

Pumpkin

Apple

1

Portrait of a Pumpkin

Draw the pumpkin. Write words that describe it.

2

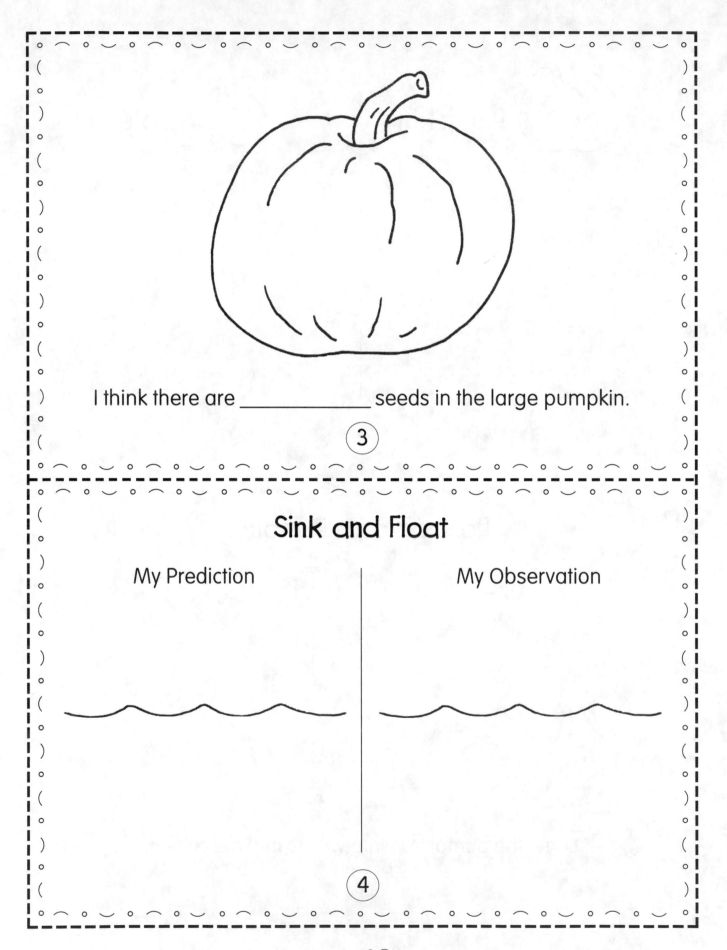

I think there are _____ seeds in the large pumpkin.

③

Sink and Float

My Prediction | My Observation

④

Bringing in the Harvest

From apples and pumpkins to peanut butter sandwiches, the activities in this section help children understand how the foods and products we use every day get from the farm to grocery stores and our homes.

SCIENCE NOTES

Getting food from the farm to the table takes almost as much energy as growing it in the first place. Nevertheless, with only 2% of the population of the United States still living on producing farms, shipping produce is a necessary fact of life. Consumers can help save energy and encourage local growing by shopping at local farmers markets and encouraging grocery stores to buy locally.

Farmer Friends

Farmers provide us with many of the products we use every day. Use a simple brown bag lunch to help children make the connection between farm and home.

Materials

◎ brown-bag lunch containing a peanut butter sandwich, apple sauce, potato chips, orange juice, paper napkin

Teaching the Lesson

1. Bring the idea of harvest home by directing students' attention to the brown-bag lunch. Explain that many of the things we eat, wear, and use come from products that farmers grow and harvest.

2. Let a few students take turns taking items out of the bag one at a time. For each item, ask: "What do you think this food is made from?" Guide children to recognize the raw harvest materials.

   ◎ peanut butter sandwich: peanuts and wheat

   ◎ orange juice: oranges

   ◎ potato chips: potatoes

   ◎ applesauce: apples

   ◎ paper bag and paper napkin: trees

3. Let children list foods they ate for lunch and discuss their origins.

 JOURNAL Junctures Reinforce the concept of food origins by having children keep food diaries at home. Ask parents to work with their children to find out the origin of the foods they eat.

 ACTIVITY Extension Peanuts are harvested but peanut butter is a processed food. Help children understand the difference between a raw, harvested food and a processed product by making peanut butter. Shell a pound of whole roasted peanuts. Place in a processor and add oil (optional) and salt (optional). Blend until smooth. Let children spread on crackers and enjoy!

Learning Center Link

Help strengthen fingers and refine fine-motor skills. Place a handheld nutcracker and a basket of unshelled peanuts and other mixed nuts in the harvest center. Invite children to use the nutcracker to shell the nuts. Encourage tasting. (Check for allergies first.) Keep a wastebasket nearby for shells.

Literature Connection Help children learn more about the way things are made with *The Tortilla Factory* by Gary Paulsen (Harcourt Brace, 1995), a life-cycle story that takes you from seed to plant to tortilla.

Harvest U.S.A.

Explore harvest near and far with this activity, beginning with harvest at home.

Materials

◎ United States map

◎ map symbols (see right)

Teaching the Lesson

1 Display a map of the United States. Have students identify their state and attach the "I live here" map symbol. Let children identify other familiar states.

2 Review the raw products from the brown-bag lunch in Farmer Friends. Explain that you purchased the items for your lunch at the grocery store. Ask: "How do you think the grocery story got these foods?" For example, children may have seen people unloading trucks at the store. Help children understand possible paths food takes. Some food, such as fresh produce, comes directly from farms. The majority of the packaged food on shelves comes from factories where raw products are made into the foods we eat.

3 Let children place the symbols on the map as follows:

◎ Peanut butter made from peanuts: Georgia

◎ Bread made from wheat: Kansas

◎ Orange juice made from oranges: Florida

◎ Potato chips made from potatoes: Idaho

◎ Paper bag made from wood: New Mexico

◎ Applesauce made from apples: Washington

4 Discuss in general terms the distance each item traveled to become a part of your lunch. Brainstorm a list of ways that food travels from its place of origin to the local grocery store—for example, trucks, trains, and airplanes.

Learning Center Link

Obtain wooden puzzles of the United States for your learning center. Some puzzles feature symbols that identify crops and resources that are produced in each state.

ACTIVITY Extension Visit a grocery store's produce department and identify fruits and vegetables. Ask for a tour of the stockroom, and request that the manager explain how the store obtains its fresh produce. What fruits and vegetables were grown locally? In other states? Other countries? Find out what happens to produce that expires. Learn more by watching *Fruit: Close Up and Very Personal* (Stagefright Productions, 1995; 800-979-6800), a wordless video about planting, processing, and consuming a great variety of fruit.

Literature Connection *Ox Cart Man* by Donald Hull (Viking, 1979) takes students back to a time when produce was grown at home and traded locally. Contrast the times of the ox cart man with modern times.

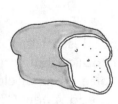

From Tree to Me

Children are the game pieces and carpet squares make up the game board in this noncompetitive, giant board game that provides counting practice and teaches how apples are transported from the tree to the lunch bag.

Materials

- 30 carpet squares (or large sheets of construction paper taped to the floor)
- masking tape
- harvest cards (see page 45)
- masking tape

Teaching the Lesson

1. In a large open space, arrange carpet squares to form three straight paths of ten mats each that lead to a finish line marked by masking tape. One child can hop along each path, so three children may play at one time.

2. Have one child stand in front of the first carpet square of each path. Read card one to the players. Continue to read the cards in order as children follow the directions and count carpet squares to move forward or back.

3. After reading the last card, have players step off the last carpet square and over the finish line. Reward each player with an apple slice or apple sticker.

4. Begin the game again with three new children.

Literature Connection Food is not the only raw product that farms produce. Some types of clothing come from farms too. Read *A New Coat for Anna*

by Harriet Ziefert (Alfred Knopf, Inc., 1986) to discover why Anna and her mother must begin at a sheep farm to get a new coat for Anna. As you read, use pictures and words to create a visual story chart that lists all the steps involved in making Anna's new coat. Design playing cards (like the ones used to play From Tree to Me; see page 45) and use them to play a giant board game based on *A New Coat for Anna*.

Learning Center Link

Draw two simple ten-square pathways on posterboard. Provide markers and the playing cards from page 45. Invite children to play From Tree to Me at the center.

From Tree to Me

1 The new apple orchard has been growing for five years and is ready to bear fruit. Move ahead 3.	**2** It is spring. Apple blossoms are on the trees. Move ahead 1.	**3** No rain for three weeks. Move back 2.
4 Honey bees visit your apple blossoms. Move ahead 3.	**5** Petals fall from the blossoms and a little green apple appears. Move ahead 1.	**6** The codling moth lays its eggs on the new fruit. Apples are in danger! Move back 2.
7 A strong wind blows apples from the trees. Move back 1.	**8** The apples reach their full size and begin to turn red. Move ahead 4.	**9** Apple pickers come today. Move ahead 2.
10 Some apples bruised by being loaded into the truck. Move back 3.	**11** Apples travel across the country in a big truck. Move ahead 4.	**12** Apples are unloaded at the store in your neighborhood. Step over the finish line!

Homemade Harvest

Wrap up your harvest unit with a celebration that lets parents and other guests share in the fun of the harvest. Scatter learning spots around the room that feature games and activities the children enjoyed in the unit. Create "Look at Me!" opportunities by proudly displaying children's harvest work. Sample the fruits of the harvest by cooking up a harvest soup. Then bring closure to the celebration by inviting children and guests alike to snuggle up while you share a memorable harvest story.

SCIENCE NOTES

All around the world, people celebrate harvest. In England some observe the "In Gathering" by making cornhusk dolls. Japan celebrates with a "Harvest Moon" festival. With the suggestions in this section, children plan their own harvest festival—complete with games, stories, special foods, and friends.

Harvest Celebration

PART 1: Design Invitations

Make invitations to send home with students. If a child is unable to bring a guest, invite an older student to come and buddy-up for the day.

To make the invitation shown here, give children red, green, or yellow construction paper. Show them how to fold the paper and cut out an apple that includes the fold and will open like an invitation.

Invite children to help decide what to write on the invitations. If possible, share sample invitations for ideas. Write the information on chart paper for students to copy.

Together, keep track of the number of invitations sent out and the responses that come in each day. For a quick math activity each day, ask children to determine how many more people need to respond.

PART 2: Plan the Party

Review some of the highlights of the harvest unit. Have students plan their festival by selecting a few activities to revisit on the big day. For example:

Play a game of tossed salad. Challenge guests to solve students' tossed salad riddles. (See pages 10–11.)

Set up a green, yellow, and red apple taste test and then chart guests' apple preferences on a graph. (See page 26.)

Lay out the felt board characters and a copy of the story *Little Green Worm Finds a*

Home. Children can retell the story for their guests. (See page 18.)

Display the poster next to the pumpkin life-cycle books. Have children explain similarities and differences to their guests.

Take a stroll down apple lane to see the large apple tree murals (see page 21), and take a peek in the classroom garden to check on the progress of pumpkin or apple seeds that are growing.

PART 3: Prepare for the Party

It's the little touches that make an occasion memorable.

Name tags: Name tags make everyone feel welcome and comfortable. Children's designs will make each one special.

Give children stick-on name tags for each guest they're expecting, plus one each for themselves. Have children write guests' names, as well as their own, on the labels and use fine-point markers to decorate with tiny pictures of harvest fruits and vegetables.

Place mats: Have each child make a place mat to transform his desk or table into a cozy place to sit and enjoy harvest treats. Break dried ears of corn into 2 1/2-inch lengths. Pour paints on paper plates. Let children roll corn cobs in paint, then roll across construction paper. Repeat, overlapping colors and designs. Set the place mats aside to dry.

PART 4: **The Big Day**

Children's work is displayed, activities have been selected and set out, name tags and place mats are waiting. Add two more activities to make your harvest festival complete. Directions for harvest soup and a keepsake (but quick) quilt follow.

TIP: *The week before the harvest party, read* Growing Vegetable Soup *by Lois Ehlert. Assign each child a vegetable to bring from home to contribute to the harvest soup.*

Hearty Harvest Soup

The morning of the harvest party (before guests arrive), make vegetable soup as a reminder of the bounty of the harvest. If your school day does not allow four hours for the soup to cook, make soup the day before and reheat on the day of the harvest festival.

Read *Growing Vegetable Soup* a second time to review the harvest process. Clean vegetables and provide plastic knives for the children to chop the vegetables they brought from home. Then follow the recipe to make vegetable soup to serve in the afternoon.

(Serves 30 people a taste of soup. Make two batches if you're expecting a crowd.)

- 2 large potatoes
- 1 onion
- 3 carrots
- 2 stalks celery
- 1 small pepper
- 1 zucchini squash
- 1 bag frozen corn
- 1 16 oz can chopped tomatoes
- 1 tbsp salt (optional)
- 3 cups water
- 3 beef bouillon cubes (optional)

Clean and chop vegetables. Put all ingredients in a Crock Pot and stir. Cover and cook on high for 4 to 5 hours. Serve.

Community Harvest Quilt

As a parting activity, invite guests and children to a cozy storytime followed by an activity for making a keepsake harvest quilt.

Materials

- *The Pumpkin Blanket* by Deborah Turney Zagwyn (Celestial Arts, 1995)
- assorted art supplies
- 8- by 8-inch squares of white construction paper
- craft paper
- packing tape

1. Read *The Pumpkin Blanket*, a delightful story about a young girl named Cleo who sacrifices her much-loved quilt to protect her garden pumpkins from an early frost.

2. Give each family a paper quilt square to decorate in a way that celebrates harvest. Have guests ask children to recount one highlight of the harvest unit and then work together to design a quilt square that expresses the harvest highlight.

3. Arrange squares on craft paper, then "stitch" with packing tape to make a quilt like Cleo's that looks surprisingly like a garden patch.

4. Display the quilt in the classroom to prompt harvest memories for months to come.